FORENSIC SCIENCE

Collecting Crime-scene Evidence

Carol Ballard

W

FRANKLIN WATTS

LONDON•SYDNEY

This edition first published in 2010
by Franklin Watts
338 Euston Road
London NW1 3BH

Franklin Watts Australia
Level 17/207 Kent Street
Sydney, NSW 2000

A CIP catalogue record for this book is
available from the British Library.

ISBN: 978 0 7496 9500 2

Dewey number: 363.2'52

Printed in Malaysia

Franklin Watts is a division of
Hachette Children's Books,
an Hachette UK company.
www.hachette.co.uk

Note to parents and teachers
concerning websites:
In the book every effort has been made by
the Publishers to ensure that websites are
suitable for children, that they are of the
highest educational value, and that they
contain no inappropriate or offensive
material. However, because of the nature of
the Internet, it is impossible to guarantee that
the contents of these sites will not be altered.
We advise that Internet access is supervised by
a responsible adult.

For The Brown Reference Group Ltd
Project Editor: Sarah Eason
Designer: Paul Myerscough
Picture Researcher: Maria Joannou
Managing Editor: Miranda Smith
Editorial Director: Lindsey Lowe
Production Director: Alastair Gourlay
Children's Publisher: Anne O'Daly

Photographic Credits:
Shutterstock: Olivier Le Queinec front cover;
Corbis: Andrew Brookes/Flirt 16, Robert
Sciarrino/ Star Ledger 28; Dreamstime: Shariff
Che'Lah 40; Fotolia: CatPaty13 26, Haemengine
21, Stepanov 17; Getty Images: Bulent Kilic/AFP
12; Istockphoto: Stefan Klein 6, Rich Legg 7,
Paul Tessier 27, Jaroslaw Wojcik 41; Science
Photo Library: Michael Donne 13, Mauro
Fermariello 34, John Mclean 39, Philippe Psaila
4, 10, Jim Varney 9; Shutterstock: Nick
Alexander 36, Gualtiero Boffi 32,
Katrina Brown 24, Kevin L Chesson 30, Dhoxax
37, Romanchuck Dimitry 22, Elisanth 15,
Laurence Gough 45, Stephen Kiers 29, Emin
Kuliyev 31, Andre Nantel 35, Olivier Le Queinec
14, Serg64 43, Kenneth Sponsler 33, Dale A
Stork 18, Stephen Sweet 5, Leah-Anne
Thompson 42, Jason Vinz 23, Klemens
Waldhuber 19; Topham Picturepoint: The
Image Works/Bob Daemmrich 8.

Contents

Hunting for clues

any criminals commit their crimes on the spur of the moment. They do not think about the clues they leave behind. A footprint in the mud, a fingerprint on a door handle or a strand of hair on the carpet – these are just some of the clues that can lead the police to a criminal. Some clues can help them to work out when and how the criminal committed the crime. By looking at all the clues, the police can sometimes piece together exactly what happened.

Forensic examiners collect evidence marked with a numbered marker at a crime scene.

12

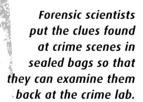

Forensic scientists put the clues found at crime scenes in sealed bags so that they can examine them back at the crime lab.

Different kinds of clue

Different crimes provide different kinds of clue. The clues might come from:

- environmental factors, such as the times of high and low tide, weather patterns or river currents
- digital equipment such as laptops and mobile phones
- footprints and other marks made by a criminal
- fibres from clothing
- weapons such as bullets and knives
- fingerprints or bite marks left by an attacker
- biological evidence such as blood, hairs or saliva
- insects such as maggots on a body
- chemicals such as cleaning fluids, drugs or poisons.

Forensic scientists examine all of the clues and provide the police with as much information as possible.

Analysis

After the crime scene has been examined, samples are taken to the crime laboratory for analysis. Eventually, the forensic scientists at the laboratory send their reports to the police. These should help the police to make sense of what happened. In many cases, the clues allow detectives to identify the criminal. Arrests can be made, and the court process can begin.

At the crime scene

When the police are called to a crime scene, they seal off the most important areas. These areas must be left untouched until they have been searched thoroughly. This is because clues could be spoiled or destroyed. For example, picking up a cup at a crime scene may smudge a fingerprint left by the criminal. Walking over soft ground could destroy a footprint. A hair from a police officer or an innocent person could be confused with one left by a criminal. To avoid losing or spoiling any clues, tape is tied around the area to mark off a crime scene.

Police tape seals off a crime scene so that the area is left undisturbed.

CROSS

CRIME SCENE DO NOT CROSS

LINE DO NOT CR

This is the primary crime scene of a murder investigation. The outline of the victim's body is marked in chalk.

Detailed procedure

When police and crime-scene investigators arrive at a crime scene, they follow certain steps:

1. Interview the first person at the scene, any other witnesses and possibly the victim to find out what happened.
2. Examine the crime scene to establish the layout and identify possible clues and evidence.
3. Photograph and record the crime scene. All the details, including the exact positions of the victim and any evidence, must be carefully noted.
4. Process the crime scene to identify and collect physical evidence for analysis at a forensic laboratory.

Crime-scene investigators

Special police officers, called crime-scene investigators, collect the evidence at a crime scene. They wear protective body suits so that the crime scene does not become contaminated. They find the clues by examining the site very carefully. If a crime took place in the open, the weather can destroy the evidence. Tents are sometimes put up to help protect outdoor crime scenes.

Primary and secondary crime scenes

There are two types of crime scene. A primary crime scene is one where the crime has actually occurred. For example, this might be where a burglary or a murder took place. A secondary crime scene is one where a suspect has been present, either before or after the crime was committed.

A police officer talks to two local people to find out about a crime that has taken place in the area.

Interview

Witnesses can tell a crime-scene investigator a great deal about a crime. Did they see anything unusual? Did they notice any strangers? Was anyone seen running away? Have there been unusual cars or bikes outside? Did they hear arguing? Did an alarm go off? Neighbours, local shopkeepers, friends and family members – all of these people may have useful information that can help the police with their investigation.

Examine

Many crime scenes are inside buildings, so the criminal must have found a way to get into the building. Are there any signs of a break-in, such as a broken window or door lock? If not, could the criminal have had a key or been let in by the victim? Is there any evidence of how the criminal left the building?

If the crime scene is outside, the crime-scene investigator makes a quick check for any disturbance on the ground. Are there any footprints or tyre tracks? Have any plants been disturbed or damaged? Has anything been dropped or left behind?

Photograph and record

Whether the crime scene is inside or outside, the crime-scene investigator must record any possible clues and evidence so that they can be examined in detail later. Photographing the crime scene is the best way to make a permanent record.

Photographs show where everything is and record important information such as whether a door is open or closed and the exact position of a victim's body. Close-up photographs can also reveal detailed information about small areas. These might show the exact position of evidence, such as a bloodstain on a wall. Other methods used for recording the crime scene include video-recording, making notes and sketching.

Process

Once everything has been recorded, the crime-scene investigators start to collect all the clues. Some items are put in bags and taken back to the crime laboratory for investigation. For example, hairs and fibres found at the crime scene are studied under a microscope. Other evidence must be processed at the crime scene. This includes fingerprints that show up when investigators apply a powder to door handles and other surfaces.

A forensic scientist carefully dusts an empty bottle with powder to reveal fingerprints left on the glass.

TRUE CRIME...

Hair evidence

In October 1994, a woman was stabbed to death. At the crime scene, investigators found a bloody baseball cap. It contained a few hairs. Police had several suspects, and samples of their hair were examined. None matched the hairs in the baseball cap. After more than a year, the murdered woman's son-in-law boasted that he had killed her. Police arrested him. When they analysed a sample of his hair, they found that it matched the hair found in the baseball cap at the crime scene. The son-in-law was sentenced to life in prison.

9

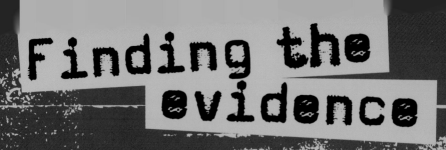

Finding the evidence

Crime-scene investigators search every part of a crime scene very carefully to look for clues. The search often starts with places that a suspect is most likely to have touched. In a burglary, for example, the criminal will probably have touched surfaces such as cupboards, doors and windows.

A crime-scene investigator finds a gun at a crime scene. It will be analysed back at the crime lab.

TRUE CRIME...

Hit and run

A car driver hit a pedestrian and drove off, leaving the victim to die. Police later arrested a suspect and searched his car. Forensic specialists examined the car's paintwork. It was blue metallic paint, with a yellow primer underneath. Then they carefully scraped the victim's clothing and collected the scrapings on a large piece of white paper. When they examined the scrapings under a microscope, they found paint flakes that seemed to match the paint on the car. To be certain they were the same, the scientists analysed the chemicals in the paint from the car and the paint from the scrapings. They were identical. This evidence helped to prove that the suspect was the hit-and-run driver.

Types of evidence

There are two main types of evidence. Physical evidence includes fingerprints and footprints, guns and bullets, and marks made by tools and other weapons. Biological evidence includes body fluids, such as blood and saliva.

Using Luminol

Luminol is a chemical that reveals traces of blood that people cannot see. Luminol glows bright blue when it reacts with blood. The chemical is not enough to confirm the presence of blood. Other tests are needed to prove it really is blood. This is because Luminol also glows blue when it mixes with other chemicals, such as bleach.

IN DEPTH

Light work

Investigators use special types of light to show different things at crime scenes. First, certain chemicals are applied to the surface that is being examined. If the surface is viewed with ultraviolet light, it may pick up blood traces, fingerprints or footprints. Fingerprints and bodily fluids such as bloodstains show up under blue light. This technique can even reveal writing that has been scribbled over.

⬆ *Forensic scientists search the site following an explosion outside a fast-food restaurant in Istanbul, Turkey.*

Search patterns

If a crime scene covers a large area, searching must be particularly methodical so that no important clues are missed. Investigators have developed several different search patterns to ensure that every search is thorough and complete:

Spiral in: A crime-scene investigator starts work at the edge of the crime scene. The investigator walks around it slowly in smaller and smaller circles until he or she reaches the centre. The investigator's steps follow a spiral pattern.

Spiral out: The crime-scene investigator starts at the centre of the scene. The investigator then walks around it slowly in bigger and bigger circles, until he or she reaches the edge. Again, the steps follow a spiral pattern.

Lines: The crime-scene investigator walks backwards and forwards in straight lines until he or she has covered the entire crime scene. The steps are in straight lines.

Parallel lines: Many crime-scene investigators walk next to each other in a straight line, from one side of the crime scene to the other. Together, their steps make a series of straight lines.

Grid: The crime-scene investigators cross the crime scene in one direction. Then they turn to walk at right angles to their first crossing. Their steps make a grid pattern.

Zone: The crime scene is divided into smaller areas. Each crime-scene investigator is given a small area in which to look for clues.

Crime-scene investigators take photos of a murder victim to record the exact position of the body.

IN DEPTH

Using photographs

Investigators can take close-up photos to record the evidence at a crime scene. This is a simple way to show other people, such as a judge and jury members, exactly what the crime scene looked like. For example, a close-up photo of drops of blood shows how many there were and how they were scattered. Investigators take photos of the evidence showing photographic scales to give an idea of the size of the blood drops.

13

There's been a murder!

A murder has been committed. The body has been removed by crime-scene investigators, and now they are searching the area thoroughly. These are the clues that they have found at the scene.

1. Broken glass on the floor below the window suggests that the suspect smashed it to get into the building. The glass is examined for clues.

2. There are drops of blood on the window frame. Bloodstains must be photographed and samples taken to the crime lab for analysis.

3. A cigarette end may have traces of saliva on it. The DNA can be extracted from it and analysed.

A special light reveals bloody fingerprints on a wall. Do they belong to the victim or the killer?

Does this button belong to a jacket worn by the killer? What type of jacket is it from? How did it fall off?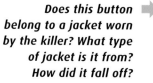

4. There's a footprint on the windowsill. Taking photographs and using an electrostatic dust lifter will help to match it to particular shoes.

5. Could there be a fingerprint on the door knob? Dusting with powder will reveal it. Then the print can be lifted with adhesive tape and attached to a card. Back at the crime lab it can be compared to fingerprints on a database of known criminals.

6. Are there any loose fibres on the rug? Using tweezers, the crime-scene investigator can pick up any fibres he or she can see. The rug can then be vacuumed to pick up any fibres that are too small to see with the naked eye.

7. There is a bullet stuck in the door frame. It must be removed very carefully. It could provide vital evidence about the type of gun from which it was fired.

8. There are two glasses on the table. Are there any traces of saliva that could be analysed? This could help to identify the two people who were drinking.

Collecting the evidence

Some evidence is fragile. It may be destroyed easily or spoil, so crime-scene investigators collect it first. Once this is done, they can collect other, more durable, evidence.

Hairs and fibres

Any hairs or fibres are picked up carefully using tweezers and put into sealed bags or containers. Some surfaces may be vacuumed so that nothing is missed. A clean bag is used for each area, so that the investigators know exactly where every tiny scrap was found.

A crime-scene ➡ *investigator picks up a hair using a pair of tweezers. The hair will be analysed back at the crime lab.*

A suspect's trainers have left an impression in the muddy ground. Investigators will take photos of the footprint and make a cast to record the evidence. ➡

Solid objects

Investigators take photographs of items such as broken glass, bullets and weapons. They put them into plastic bags so that they cannot be damaged and attach labels so that they can be identified when they are examined at the lab.

Making casts

If a footprint is found in mud, investigators take photographs of it. Next, they make a permanent model, called a cast, of the footprint. To do this, the investigators mix casting material and water to make a dough-like mixture. They pour this material into the footprint in the mud. The cast is left until it fully hardens. Then it is lifted out carefully, put in a box and taken back to the lab.

IN DEPTH

Body fluids

Some items may contain traces of body fluids, such as blood or saliva. For example, a dirty glass could have traces of saliva on it. This could yield a substance called DNA, which is found in every part of the body. Every person's DNA is unique. This means that the DNA found at a crime scene can be used as evidence to link a person to it. Items that might yield traces of body fluids are gently wiped with cotton swabs to soak up any fluid present. The swabs are taken back to the crime lab for analysis.

Fingerprints

Suspects leave fingerprints on many different surfaces. Some are visible, such as those left by a blood-soaked hand on the smooth surface of a wall. Fingerprints can also be left on a softer surface, such as soap. An indentation may be visible, but not the fine details. Fingerprints left by sweat on a smooth surface cannot always be seen by the naked eye. Investigators use other techniques to see these prints.

A fingerprint is lifted from a surface using clear adhesive tape. The print will be transferred to a special type of card to make it more visible.

Finding prints

Crime-scene investigators look for fingerprints on surfaces such as doors and handles. It is highly likely that a suspect has touched these surfaces. Sometimes, shining a bright light on a surface can make the print visible. It becomes difficult to see when the light is switched off. Methods have been developed to make a permanent record of prints such as these.

Fingerprints can be used to confirm the identity of a suspect.

19

IN DEPTH

Collecting prints

Investigators use one of several different techniques to make fingerprints more visible:

Powder can be brushed onto a surface. It sticks to the print, making it visible. The powder can be black, silver or some other colour that contrasts with the surface. A photograph of the print is taken. Cellophane is placed over the print. The tape is removed, lifting the print with it. The tape is then stuck onto a card of a contrasting colour to the powder.

Chemicals, such as iodine, ninhydrin or silver nitrate, can be used to reveal prints on porous materials. The chemical can be sprayed onto the surface of the material, or the material can be dipped into the liquid chemical. The chemical makes any fingerprints become visible.

Fumes, such as those from a special glue, can make a print visible without damaging the object on which it is found. The glue is heated on a metal plate. The plate and the object on which the print is found are put into an airtight container. The fumes from the glue react with the prints to make them visible.

Clues in the environment

The environment can provide a lot of information about a crime. Sometimes it can confirm that a suspect's story is true. Sometimes it can prove that a suspect is lying. It can also help the police to locate a body or other items.

TRUE CRIME...

Pine-tree seeds

In 1960, the body of Graeme Thorne was discovered. On his body, forensic examiners found seeds from a rare pine tree. There were no pine trees of that type near the place where the body was found. The seeds appeared to be a clue. Police searched for a pine tree that could have yielded the seeds and they found one in a nearby garden. They also found that the mortar between the bricks of the house matched mortar dust found on the body. With these separate clues, the police were able to identify the murderer and secure a conviction in court.

Weather evidence

Meteorologists know what the weather was like at a certain place and time. This can help the police to confirm a suspect's story. For example, a suspect may say that her car skidded on ice. The expert may say that it was too warm for the road to be icy. This would suggest that the suspect is lying.

Soil evidence

Soil has different features depending on its source. A suspect's shoes may have soil traces. Analysing the soil can then provide evidence that the suspect has visited a place.

Tides and currents

If a body is thrown into a river, the current will carry it away. Knowing the speed and direction of the current can help the police in two ways. If they know where and when something entered the river, it can help them to find it. Or if they find the body, it can help them to work out exactly where it was thrown in.

Tides can provide similar information. High and low tides occur twice a day. The timing of the tides can provide useful information in a police search.

Plant evidence

Traces of plant matter can be analysed and linked to places where that type of plant grows. For example, finding hazel pollen on a person's clothes shows that he or she has been in an area where hazel trees grow. Plants at the crime scene can also yield clues. They may have been trampled on, or low branches may have been broken.

When magnified by a microscope, traces of tiny pollen grains on a person's clothes can reveal where he or she has been.

EXAMINE THE EVIDENCE

Soil types

Collect a few soil samples from different locations, such as a field and a garden. Put each soil sample in a separate plastic bag. When you have collected the samples, tip each one onto a tray and compare them. Differences such as colour, texture and the presence of stones or dead plant matter can reveal differences between the soil from different places.

Digital evidence

Computers reveal all sorts of information that can help the police to solve crimes. Detectives may need to search laptops and PCs, as well as places where data may be stored, such as CDs, memory cards or the Internet. Depending on how many officers are available, and how much material must be searched, the length of an investigation can vary from a few days to several months.

22

↓ *The forensic examination of computer equipment is central to many criminal cases.*

Hiding information

Information is often hidden to make it more difficult for the police to find. Files are protected by passwords. They can also be encrypted, so that they can be read only by using the software that decodes them. People may delete files to prevent them from being read, but it is almost impossible to remove all traces of them. Experts can still access the files. Some criminals use 'anti-forensics' software. This makes it much more difficult for detectives to access the information on a computer.

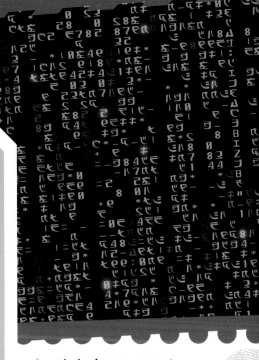

Criminals may encrypt files to prevent the police from looking at them.

23

A careful process

Forensic examiners locate all the files on a computer. They track websites and e-mails. They keep a record of everything that they do so that they can prove that their actions have not changed the computer in any way.

Digital clues

Other electronic equipment can yield information. Mobile phones store contact details. Companies that make mobile phones keep records of where the phones are when calls are made. These details provide important clues for police investigating a crime.

On the Internet

Internet companies keep detailed records about their customers' Internet use. This includes details of all the websites they visit, how often they visit them and how long they spend on each site. This information can be extremely useful to criminal investigators. For example, a computer that has been used to look at the websites of terrorist groups may link the owner to terrorist activities.

Clues from marks

Different types of marks reveal important information about a crime. Bullet holes, footprints and tyre and tool marks are all evidence of what happened and who was involved.

Footprints

Footprints are left in one of two ways. If someone stands in something soft, such as sand or soil, his or her weight pushes down. The shape and distinctive tread patterns of the shoes become visible. If someone treads in something sticky, wet or powdery, it clings to the shoes. When he or she walks on another surface, a footprint is left behind. Forensic scientists take photos and make casts of these footprints to record the evidence.

Tyres leave tracks in the sand. Forensic experts take photos to keep a record of tyre tracks.

Tyre tracks

Tyre tracks are left in the same ways as footprints. Driving through mud leaves tracks in the mud. Driving onto a road transfers some mud to the road, again leaving marks. Photos and casts of these tracks can be compared with the tyres of a suspect's vehicle.

Tool marks

Criminals use tools to break into houses and vehicles. A tool makes a mark when it moves across a surface. Several factors affect the mark that is made. A screwdriver and a knife have edges with different shapes, and they leave marks with different shapes. The surface on which the tool is used is important, too, as a tool leaves a bigger mark on a soft surface than on a harder surface. Another factor is the force used to make the mark. The stronger the force, the bigger the mark is likely to be. The way the tool is moved also affects the type of mark made. A single stabbing movement makes a narrow, deep hole. A sideways movement makes a long, shallow scratch.

Bullet holes

Bullet holes can help forensic scientists to work out from which direction the bullet was fired. Scientists can work out the height the gun was at and the height of the person holding it when it was fired. Sometimes a bullet is found in a wall or door frame. Digging it out might damage the bullet, so a chunk of the wall or frame is cut out, with the bullet still in it. The bullet is removed carefully at the crime lab.

EXAMINE THE EVIDENCE

Look at your footprints

Have a close look at your own footprints. Put a clean sheet of paper on a hard floor. The paper should be bigger than your feet. Put on a pair of shoes with a clear pattern on the sole. Go outside and stand in a muddy area, then put one foot on the paper. Press down firmly and then lift your foot. There should be a clear footprint on the paper. Try this with some friends and compare the footprints. Can you identify each person's shoes?

25

Clues from weapons

Finding a weapon can be a major breakthrough in solving a crime such as murder. The weapon can often reveal a lot of information.

Weapons of all kinds

Many different objects can be used as weapons. Some criminals carry weapons with the intent of committing a crime. Everyday items are also picked up on the spur of the moment and used as weapons. For example, a baseball bat can be grabbed during an argument and used to hit someone.

Using weapons to catch a criminal

Weapons can help the police to identify a criminal. This might be directly, for example using the documents you need to own a firearm. Sometimes the criminal may leave evidence, such as a fingerprint or a trace of DNA, on a weapon dropped at the crime scene.

Forensic experts can tell a lot about the shape of a knife used by a criminal by looking at the victim's stab wounds.

Using ballistics

Forensic ballistics is the study of ammunition and the marks that guns make on the ammunition when it is fired. The barrel of a gun makes scratches and marks on every bullet that is fired. Most guns make patterns on the ammunition that are different from other guns. Investigators may be able to match a bullet to the gun that fired it. Recently, though, some people have questioned whether ballistics evidence is always accurate.

27

Weapons can also link a criminal to a crime. It is often possible to identify the gun from which a bullet was fired. The police can compare a bullet found at a crime scene to a bullet fired from the suspect's gun. If the two match, it is likely that the suspect was involved in the shooting.

Stab wounds can reveal a lot about the type of weapon that caused the mark. The shape of the blade, including its width and length, can be worked out by studying the wounds. This can help police to narrow down the search for the weapon. It can also be used to determine whether or not a particular weapon could have caused the injuries.

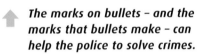

The marks on bullets – and the marks that bullets make – can help the police to solve crimes.

TRUE CRIME...

Ballistics history

Ballistics evidence was first used in a murder case in 1902. The expert witness, Oliver Wendell Holmes Jr, fired a bullet from a suspect's gun into a wad of cotton. He then examined the bullet and compared it to the one that had killed the victim. The marks on the bullets were identical, and the court found the suspect guilty of murder.

Fingerprints and bites

No one has yet found two sets of fingerprints that are the same, so fingerprints can be used to help the police identify a suspect or a victim.

Fingerprints

Crime-scene investigators collect all the fingerprints they can find at a crime scene. They also take prints from suspects and see if they match those from the crime scene. Matching prints is good evidence that the suspect was at the crime scene. Police keep records of the prints of known criminals on a computer database for use when fingerprints are found at a crime scene.

A US police officer takes fingerprints from a suspect. The prints will be stored on a computer database.

If police do not already have a suspect, they can try to match the prints with those on the database.

Bites

Bite marks on skin can be recorded and compared with photographs of a suspect's teeth. They can also be compared with a cast of a suspect's bite. The features that are compared include the size and shape of the jaws, any missing teeth and teeth that are broken. This provides the evidence that will help to prove innocence or guilt. Everybody's teeth are different, and jaw sizes vary. So each person's bite mark is unique and can be used for identification.

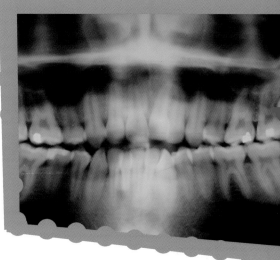

Forensic experts compare bite marks to dental records to identify a suspect.

IN DEPTH

Animal teeth

Animal bite marks can be used to help solve crimes. The jaws of different animals come in different shapes and sizes and with different numbers and arrangements of teeth. A cat's jaws and teeth, for example, are different from a dog's. When a person is killed by a wild animal, investigators examine the bite marks to find out what type of animal was responsible for the death. They may even be able to tell if the animal was young or old.

EXAMINE THE EVIDENCE

Make your own fingerprints

You can make your own fingerprints. Rub a soft pencil on a piece of paper to make a dark area. Rub one of your fingertips over this area until it becomes grey. Then stick a piece of clear adhesive tape on your fingertip. Pull it off slowly and stick it onto a piece of plain white paper. Your fingerprint will show up clearly!

Biological evidence

Biological evidence at a crime scene comes from many different sources. Some evidence, such as hairs and spots of blood, is obvious. Other evidence may be less obvious, or even invisible to the naked eye, but it is no less important.

Sources

Where should a crime-scene investigator look for biological evidence? The chart on the next page shows a few possible sources, exactly where to look on those sources and what type of evidence might be found.

⬇ *The saliva taken from a suspect could match saliva found at a crime scene.*

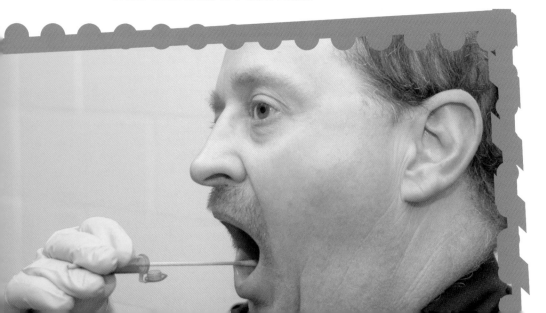

Serology

The study of blood is called serology. Blood contains serum. It also contains red and white blood cells. Serum and red blood cells can provide vital information about a blood sample.

- **Serum** can help to identify a person. Scientists study substances in serum, called antibodies, that the body makes to fight disease. If they are found, it shows that the person has had a particular illness at some point in his or her life. This can be crucial in identifying an individual. Even identical twins, with identical DNA, will have different serum antibodies.

- **Red blood cells** can be used to find out a person's blood group. Human blood belongs to one of four groups: A, B, AB or O. Human blood is also grouped as either Rhesus Positive (+) or Rhesus Negative (-).

31

Many people share the same blood group, but analysing blood can still narrow down the list of potential suspects.

Source	Where will the evidence be?	What evidence could be found?
dirty clothes	anywhere on the surface	sweat, traces of skin, hairs
used stamp or envelope	licked part of the stamp	saliva
hat	inside	sweat, hair, dandruff
bottle, cup of glass	around the rim or sides	saliva, sweat, oil from skin
spectacles	nose pieces, ear pieces	sweat, traces of skin
mobile phone	anywhere on the surface	sweat, skin, saliva

DNA evidence

DNA evidence was first introduced in the 1980s. Since then it has been used in many different countries to solve a wide range of crimes.

What is DNA?

Gathering DNA evidence involves complex scientific processes, but the idea behind it is very simple. The body of every living thing is made up of millions of tiny cells. Cells are too small to be seen with the naked eye. Scientists look at cells through microscopes. Under a microscope, you can see an even smaller nucleus at the centre of each cell. The nucleus contains the blueprint for life in the form of coded instructions called genes. People inherit genes from their parents. Genes determine everything, from the colour of your eyes to how tall you will be.

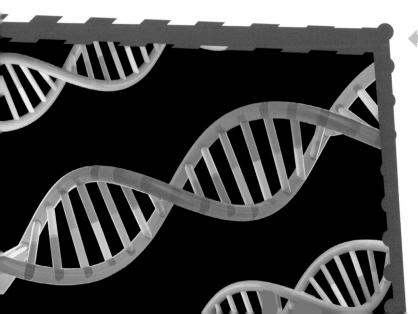

A molecule of DNA looks like a twisted ladder. This shape is called a double helix.

Examining DNA can determine if two people are related. The DNA of these identical twins will be an exact match.

DNA is short for deoxyribonucleic acid. This chemical carries the genetic code. The only people known to have exactly the same DNA are identical twins. This means that analysing a sample of DNA evidence can be used for identification. There are some similarities between the DNA profiles of individuals in a family. This means that DNA can also be used to prove whether or not two people are related.

Sources of DNA

DNA can be found in tiny samples of biological evidence such as hairs, skin cells or spots of blood. Recently, scientists have found a way to obtain a DNA profile from even smaller sources than was previously possible. This is called low copy number (LCN) analysis. However, the results from this new method may not always be correct, and scientists are still developing the technique.

TRUE CRIME...

DNA database

In August 1999, two students at Virginia University were asleep when an intruder attacked them, threatened them with a gun and stole items from their room. Traces of saliva found on a beer can near the crime scene were analysed. However, the DNA profile did not match anyone the police suspected of the crime. Then, in October 1999, a match was found on the police database with the DNA profile of a criminal called Montaret D. Davis. He was put on trial and convicted on the basis of the DNA evidence.

DNA testing

A crime has been committed. The police have a suspect, and they have collected a sample of saliva from his mouth. His DNA will be analysed. These are the main steps in the testing process.

1. A crime-scene investigator notices an object at the crime scene. It may have DNA on it, so she takes a photograph to record the evidence. She puts the sample in a container, seals it and labels it carefully, recording where she found it.

2. The sample is sent to the crime lab. The sample should be kept cool and away from direct sunlight. This is because high temperatures can damage or destroy the DNA.

34

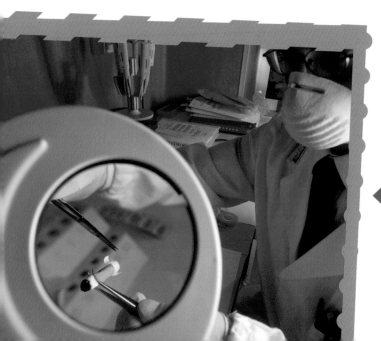

← *Saliva on the end of a cigarette end can be used to build up a DNA profile.*

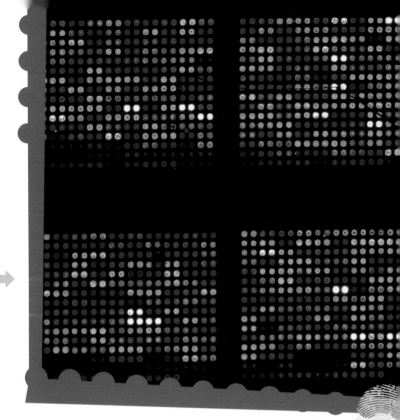

DNA profiles are held on computer databases. Forensic experts search these databases to match with DNA found at a crime scene.

3. Back at the lab, the DNA is extracted from the sample. The amount of DNA is measured and recorded.

4. The pure sample of DNA is then analysed. A technique called gel electrophoresis separates the DNA into a column with a series of stripes, like a bar code. This pattern is called the DNA profile.

5. The DNA profile from the crime scene is then compared with the suspect's DNA profile.

6. A match between the suspect's DNA profile and the DNA profile from the crime scene may be sufficient evidence to link the suspect to the crime.

7. If there is no suspect, or if the suspect's DNA profile does not match the profile from the crime scene, police search databases containing DNA profiles of known criminals. A match on the database indicates that the criminal may have been at the crime scene.

Looking at bodies

When a body is found, police need to find out how the person died. Was it the result of illness or an accident, or was it murder or suicide? The body can provide a lot of information to help answer these questions. Bodies are examined by specially trained doctors called forensic pathologists. The examination is called a post mortem.

The body itself is an invaluable source of evidence. It is stored in a cool mortuary to preserve vital clues.

Body processes

Some body processes, such as breathing, stop after people die. Imagine a body is pulled from a river. If the lungs are full of water, it suggests that the person drowned. This could have been an unfortunate accident. If the lungs are not full of water, the body entered the water after death. This is very suspicious.

What can a body reveal?

From a post mortem, a forensic pathologist may be able to work out when a person died and what killed him or her. Extra information, such as the type of weapon used in a murder, or whether the victim had been drinking alcohol, can be established. It may also be possible to tell whether a body was moved after death.

Serious damage to a person's skull suggests that he or she died from a head wound.

37

How is a post mortem carried out?

Photographs are taken at every step of the post mortem. They may be used as evidence. The first step is to look for clues on the skin. There might be bruises or other injuries. If a victim tried to fight off an attack, flakes of the attacker's skin might be under the fingernails. Teeth can be compared with dental records to confirm the person's identity.

Next, the internal organs are removed, weighed and studied for signs of injury. Samples of blood are sent to the forensic laboratory. The blood is tested for drugs, poisons and other chemicals that might have caused death.

IN DEPTH

Bones speak

This table shows some of the questions that can be answered by examining bones:

Question	From where?	How?
how old was the person when he or she died?	skull	older people have smoother skulls; the bones of a child's skull are not completely joined together
male or female?	skull and pelvis	men have more prominent brows, jawbones and eye sockets; women have a wider pelvis
how tall?	thigh bone	this is usually about one-quarter of an adult's height
how heavy?	whole skeleton	skeletons of heavier people show more signs of wear
right-handed or left-handed?	arms and shoulders	the dominant side has stronger muscle attachments
occupation?	whole skeleton	look for job-related changes or damage – for example, a trumpet player's teeth may be distorted
ethnic group?	nose shape	differs between groups
violent death?	whole skeleton	signs of injury or struggle include damage to the skull, broken bones, bullet damage

Reconstructing the past

When a human body is found a long time after death, a normal post mortem cannot be done. The remains are too badly decayed. Sometimes only a skeleton remains. Forensic anthropologists are experts in studying these remains. They can still find out a lot about the body to help to identify the dead person. Forensic artists can recreate the person's face.

IN DEPTH

A face from the past

Tutankhamun was an Egyptian pharaoh. He ruled between 1336 and 1327 BCE but died when he was only 19 years old. Like all the Egyptian pharaohs, the body of Tutankhamun was preserved as a mummy and buried in a tomb.

Over 3,000 years later, a British archaeologist named Howard Carter discovered the tomb hidden in the Valley of the Kings. When he looked inside, Carter found Tutankhamun's mummy with a beautiful golden mask over his face. Still, no one knew what his actual face looked like.

In 2007, a team of forensic artists from France, Egypt and the United States decided to reconstruct Tutankhamun's face using detailed scans of his skull. The models made show that the pharaoh had rounded cheeks, a sloping nose and a round chin. At last, we know what Tutankhamun looked like.

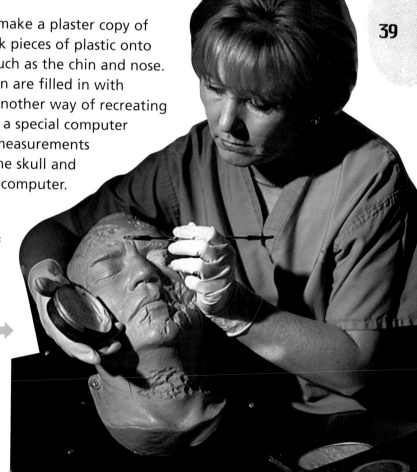

Sometimes they make a plaster copy of the skull and stick pieces of plastic onto it at key points such as the chin and nose. The gaps between are filled in with modelling clay. Another way of recreating the face is to use a special computer program. Many measurements are taken from the skull and processed by the computer. The program will then create an approximation of the person's face.

Forensic artists use their knowledge of anatomy to reconstruct a person's face from his or her skull.

39

Clues from insects

After a person dies, his or her body begins to decay. The process can be slowed if the body is kept cool. Otherwise, decay is rapid. As the body decays, insects are attracted to it. Insects can provide clues about the time of death. Insect investigations are done by scientists called forensic entomologists.

Types of insect

The types of insect involved vary depending on the climate and country. The first to arrive are flies. Blowflies, houseflies and scavenger flies are just some of the species that appear. They lay eggs on the dead body, and the eggs develop into maggots. Scientists have studied the life cycles of different flies. They

Insects help investigators to work out the time of a person's death.

know exactly how many days it takes for the maggots to develop. They can also identify how many generations of flies and maggots have been on the body. This can help them to work out the time of death.

Beetles arrive later in the decaying process. Most beetles lay their eggs in the body, and the larvae that emerge feed on the flesh. Hide beetles come late in the decaying process. They feed on bone, dried skin and hair.

Mites can arrive at any stage to feed on dried skin. Some hitch a ride with the beetles. Moths are some of the last insects to arrive. They feed on hair and add to the final stages of decay.

Some insects can cause problems for forensic scientists. Some feed on the body, while others eat the eggs and maggots. This makes it hard to work out the time of death. If the maggots have been eaten, vital information about the generations may be missing.

Flies lay their eggs on dead bodies. The eggs hatch into maggots, which feed on the rotting flesh.

TRUE CRIME...

Blowfly evidence

The body of a girl was found in Lydney, England, in June 1961. After looking at the level of decay of the body, police thought that the murder had taken place six to eight weeks earlier. They were puzzled because several witnesses said that they had seen the victim much later than this. Then Keith Simpson, the forensic entomologist, said that the blowfly maggots he found were just nine to twelve days old. The police used this information to work out the time of death and find the girl's murderer. He was found guilty based on the blowfly evidence.

Chemical clues

re traces of powder evidence of illegal drugs? Was a fire started by lighting a petrol-soaked rag? Chemicals are often found at a crime scene – providing clues about the victim, the suspect and the way in which the crime was committed.

Forensic toxicologists

Scientists who study chemicals, especially poisons, are called forensic toxicologists. They try to identify the chemicals, their strength and their effects on people. Forensic toxicologists also study blood or urine samples to test for drugs or poisons.

Simple tests are done first to narrow down the types of chemical in the sample. Toxicologists then do more detailed tests to find out exactly which substances are present and how much there is of each one. Most samples are tested in two different ways.

Police need to identify the chemicals present at a crime scene. Forensic toxicologists can help the police to answer these questions.

Hair evidence

Hair can contain traces of drugs and other substances that have been consumed, either over a long time or in high doses. Hair grows at a rate of about 1cm (0.5in) a month. Testing at a number of different places along the hair's length can indicate when a substance may have been consumed.

Forensic toxicologists test *the body for many different drugs, from prescription medicines to illegal drugs.*

This is because it is more convincing if results from two different tests are the same. It proves that the substance is present in the sample and not there as the result of a laboratory error.

Poison victim

In suspected poisonings, body samples are taken away for testing. In murder cases, samples are routinely tested as part of the post mortem, even if poison is not suspected. Back at the lab, the samples are treated to extract and purify the poisons. Some poisons are extracted using chemicals such as chloroform. Techniques called mass spectrometry and chromatography are used to separate different chemicals and then identify them. If a poisonous substance is found in a sample, police know they are looking for a murderer.

TRUE CRIME... 43

Tylenol™

In September 1982, Mary Kellermann took a capsule of a drug called Tylenol™. Soon afterwards, she became ill and died. During the next few days, six more people died after taking Tylenol™. Forensic toxicologists analysed the capsules and found that they had been contaminated with a poison called potassium cyanide. The medicine was removed from pharmacies. The work of the toxicologists prevented anyone else from dying. The police found out what had happened, but they never discovered who had contaminated the capsules.

Careers in forensics

What would it be like to work as a forensic scientist? Probably two facts that everyone in the field would agree on is that every day of their working life is different and that they never know what is going to happen in the laboratory next.

CSIs

Crime-scene investigators (CSIs) collect the clues that are later analysed by forensic specialists. CSIs often work long hours, and they have to deal with some grisly crime scenes. If you do not like the sight of blood, then this is not the job for you! Most CSIs first join a police force. Once they have trained as police officers, they have more specialist training to become a CSI. The entry requirements are different in different places. Many CSIs have a university degree, but many do not.

SALARY CHART

This chart shows what a forensic scientist can expect to earn if he or she takes up these specialisms as a career.

Forensic scientist	Approximate salary per year
CSI	£40,000
Forensic pathologist	£47,000
Forensic toxicologist	£40,000

Forensic scientists

You will need several important qualities to work in a forensic laboratory. To succeed, you need to be able to:

- work accurately, carrying out scientific tests reliably and to the highest standards
- be methodical and logical in the way you work so that you do not mix up samples or results
- be good at mathematics and computing so that you can analyse your data and write reports
- have a good understanding of one or more basic science subjects.

If this sounds like you, why not think about a career in forensic science? Many universities offer special degrees in forensic science. Entry requirements vary, but for most having a science background is necessary.

Specialists

Many forensic scientists decide to specialise in one area of forensic science, such as forensic anthropology, pathology, toxicology, serology or entomology. Some specialists train in their own subject area and then have further training to apply their knowledge to forensic science. Sometimes they learn by working alongside experienced professionals.

For example, a forensic pathologist first trains and works as a doctor. After a few years, he or she can then train to become a forensic pathologist.

Forensic work involves a lot of lab testing, so it helps to have a background in science.

45

Glossary

antibodies – Chemicals made by the body in response to germs.

ballistics – Study of firearms and bullets.

cast – Model of something.

chromatography – Method used to separate out the different chemicals in a substance.

contaminated – Made impure or unsafe by contact with other substances.

database – Collection of information, usually stored on a computer.

decay – To become decomposed; to rot away.

DNA – Genetic material that carries the code that determines the make-up of every living thing.

encrypted – Written in code.

fibre – Fine strand of material.

forensic anthropologist – Scientist who studies the origin and development of human beings.

forensic artist – Person who creates portraits based on forensic evidence.

forensic entomologist – Scientist specialising in the study of insects that feed on dead bodies.

forensic scientist – Person who uses science or technology to investigate and establish facts in a criminal case.

forensic toxicologist – Scientist specialising in the study of poisons in dead bodies.

gel electrophoresis – Method used in the analysis of DNA.

gene – Segment of DNA that contains the code for a trait such as blood type or eye colour.

larva – Stage of insect development between egg and pupa.

maggot – Wormlike stage in the life cycle of flies.

mass spectrometry – Method used for analysing and separating chemicals.

mortar – Mixture of material used to glue bricks together in buildings.

organ – Part of the body such as the heart, lungs or brain.

pathologist – Doctor who studies human remains to help work out the cause of death.

pollen – Fine powder made by flowers and used in fertilisation.

porous – Able to absorb liquids.

post mortem – Examination of a dead body to find out the cause of death.

saliva – Liquid produced by glands in the mouth to keep it moist.

serology – Study of blood and other body fluids.

Further reading

Books

Dowen, Elizabeth. *What's it Like to be a Forensic Scientist?* London: A & C Black Publishers, 2009.

Hopping, Lorraine. *Be a Crime Scene Investigator.* Tunbridge Wells, Kent: ticktock Media Ltd, 2008.

Rose, Malcolm and Hill, Dave. *Scene of the Crime: A Forensic Mystery Where You Crack the Case.* London: Kingfisher, 2008.

Scott, Carey. *Crime Scene Detective.* London: Dorling Kindersley, 2007.

Websites

Find out how crime-scene investigations work at the How Stuff Works website:

http://science.howstuffworks.com/csi.htm

This site features information about forensic and crime-scene investigations – plus a mystery to solve:

www.abc.net.au/science/slab/forensic/default.htm

Find a database of forensic science facts, a timeline showing important forensic events and a game to play at:

www.virtualmuseum.ca/Exhibitions/Myst/en/rcmp/index.html

Index